DIMINISHED**GUITAR**
SCALE MASTERY

Discover Game-Changing Soloing Approaches with the Diminished Scale for Guitar

LEVI**CLAY**

FUNDAMENTAL**CHANGES**

Diminished Guitar Scale Mastery

Discover Game-Changing Soloing Approaches with the Diminished Scale for Guitar

ISBN: 978-1-78933-435-7

Published by **www.fundamental-changes.com**

Copyright © 2024 Levi Clay

Edited by Tim Pettingale

www.fundamental-changes.com

For over 350 free guitar lessons with videos check out:

www.fundamental-changes.com

Join our free Facebook Community of Cool Musicians

www.facebook.com/groups/fundamentalguitar

Tag us for a share on Instagram: **FundamentalChanges**

Cover Image Copyright: Shutterstock, PrinceOfLove

Contents

Get the Audio 4

Introduction 5

Chapter One – Whole-Half Diminished Scale 6

Chapter Two – Half-Whole Diminished Scale 17

Chapter Three – Sequence Practice 27

Chapter Four – Diminished Arpeggios 34

Chapter Five – Pattern Based Playing 44

Chapter Six – Common Jazz Sequences 54

Chapter Seven – Triad Pairs 62

Chapter Eight – Advanced Triad Concepts 68

Chapter Nine – Resolving Diminished Lines 74

Chapter Ten – Diminished Sounds… Just Because 83

Conclusion – What's Next? 90

Get the Audio

The audio files for this book are available to download for free from **www.fundamental-changes.com**. The link is in the top right-hand corner. Click "Download Audio" and choose your instrument. Select the title of this book from the menu, and complete the form to get your audio.

We recommend that you download the files directly to your computer (not to your tablet or phone) and extract them there before adding them to your media library. If you encounter any difficulty, we provide technical support within 24 hours via the contact form.

For over 350 free guitar lessons with videos check out:

www.fundamental-changes.com

Join our free Facebook Community of Cool Musicians

www.facebook.com/groups/fundamentalguitar

Tag us for a share on Instagram: **FundamentalChanges**

Introduction

Over the last few hundred years, musicians and composers have continued to push the boundaries of scale knowledge and their application in music harmony to uncover exciting new sounds. Look at the history of western classical music, from the renaissance era forwards, and you'll see a constant evolution. From the rudimentary exploration of modal sounds and V-I-based functional harmony, through to extended harmony, pentatonics, chromaticism, serialism, and beyond, music is no different than art.

The most creative people are always looking for ways to express something new and exciting, rather than repeating what went before, so after exhausting the fundamental sounds, musicians went in search of more exotic sounds. Some explored the melodic minor scale, harmonic major modes, and whole tone and augmented scales. Others turned to creating modified pentatonic scales. There are lots of avenues we can explore, but I've always been a fan of the two incarnations of the diminished scale.

Why Diminished?

Why do I need to know this scale? you might ask.

The diminished scale is an incredibly useful device to instantly spice up your musical vocabulary, and is a genre-crossing tool that has been used equally in rock, blues, jazz, fusion and more. Exponents include players such as Josh Smith, Robben Ford, Mike Stern, Oz Noy, Carl Verheyen, Allan Holdsworth, John McLaughlin… the list goes on!

For many guitar players, however, the diminished scale remains a mysterious, out-of-bounds area. We know it has great musical potential, but we're afraid to *really* engage with it. Hence, this book. Here, you'll learn how the diminished scale is constructed, learn the most useful ways of playing it, learn musical sequences with it, and above all discover how to apply it musically.

To get the most from this book, I'm assuming you have a solid knowledge of simple concepts like the major scale and its modes, pentatonic scales, and how chords are formed. I'm not talking about complete *mastery* of these concepts – few of us will ever achieve that – but you should understand concepts such as the difference between major and minor scales, know the diatonic chords belonging to the major scale, understand where dominant 7 chords want to resolve to, etc. Knowledge of such theory is not essential, but it will make this book easier to understand.

This book is the result of many years of fascination with the diminished scale. I hope you enjoy studying it as much as I've enjoyed putting it together for you.

Levi

Chapter One – Whole-Half Diminished Scale

The diminished scale has a long history and has been known by many names including the Octatonic scale, Messiaen's Second Mode of Limited Transposition (after French composer Olivier Messiaen), Pijper's scale (after Dutch composer Willem Pijper), Modus Conjunctus (the choice of Anthon van der Horst), the Half-Whole or Whole-Half Diminished scale, and the Auxiliary Diminished!

I like to avoid musical terms that aren't completely descriptive, so I prefer the Whole-Half Diminished scale (and the Half-Whole Diminished, which we'll look at in Chapter Two). These names tell us something about the intervals of the scale and give us a clue about how they might be used.

Diminished scales are *symmetrical* scales, meaning that they are constructed from a pattern that repeats. As its name implies, the Whole-Half Diminished scale is constructed from a series of alternating whole steps and half steps.

If we start the scale on the note E, we'll then move a whole step to the note F#, then a half step to G, then a whole step to A, and so on.

To get familiar with the pattern, we'll apply it to a single string and play it on the first string.

Example 1a

We can apply the whole step-half step pattern to any string, so this time let's play it on the second string, starting on the E note at the 5th fret.

Example 1b

Or we can jump over to the fourth string.

Example 1c

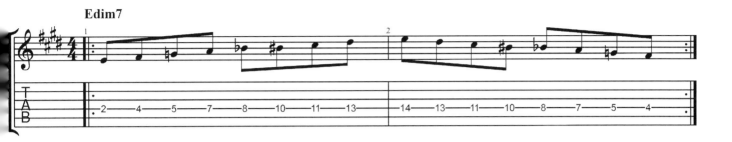

It's good to learn scales along one string because it helps us to embed the intervals in our ears and visualise the pattern, but it's impractical to play them like this, so let's look at some useful scale shapes.

Play Example 1d and you'll see a wonderful pattern happening as we play E Whole-Half Diminished in two octaves, ascending and descending. With each finger assigned to consecutive frets, use fingers 1 3 4 on the low E string, then fingers 1 2 4 on the A string. This pattern repeats across the strings, which is incredibly helpful for learning it.

Example 1d

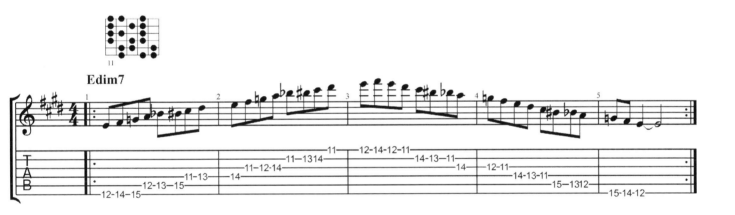

The unique construction of the diminished scale means that it repeats in minor 3rds. In other words, the E Whole-Half Diminished scale contains the same notes as G Whole-Half Diminished (a minor 3rd jump) and also Bb and Db Whole-Half Diminished scales.

Guitar players don't often think in terms of note names (me included), so it's probably easier to remember that any diminished scale pattern you know can be moved up or down the fretboard in three-fret intervals and you'll be playing all the right notes, just in a different order.

Let's try that now by playing the same pattern as the previous example, but moving it up to begin from the G note on the sixth string, 3rd fret. The example is played over an Edim7 chord. Although we're playing the pattern of the G Whole-Half Diminished scale, it's still the same as E Whole-Half Diminished when played over that chord – the scales have identical notes.

Example 1e

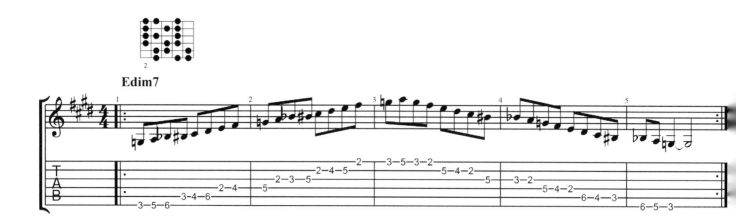

The previous example was a wonderful position-based fingering, but there's another common fingering pattern that moves across the entire neck in a four-note per string pattern, which is great for position shifting.

Don't try to play each string with four different fingers, however. Instead, use the first, second and fourth fingers, then slide up to play the last note on each string also with the fourth finger.

On the way down, use the fourth, third and first fingers, then slide down to play the last note on each string also with the first finger.

I've indicated the slides in the TAB. These are shift slides not legato slides, so both notes are picked. We're just fretting both notes with the same finger!

Example 1f

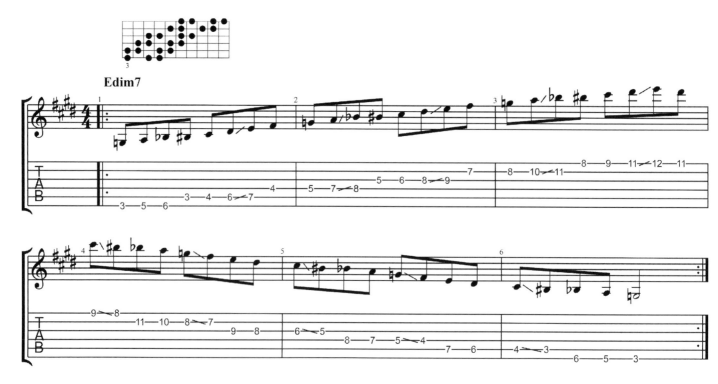

The biggest blessing of the diminished scale (its symmetrical fingerings) can also be its biggest curse, because there are so many ways to play this scale with its repeating patterns.

Here's how I like to finger the Whole-Half Diminished scale when I play it from a root note on the fifth string. This pattern uses a combination of three and four notes per string, and is played in position.

Example 1g

Here's a similar idea, this time starting on the sixth string. It begins on a Bb note, so can be viewed as the Bb Whole-Half Diminished scale (which, as we've discovered, contains identical notes to E Whole-Half Diminished).

Example 1h

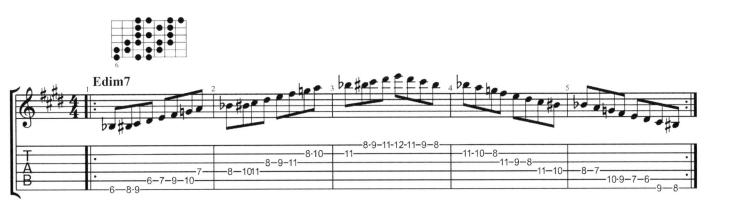

The more we get to grips with these patterns, the easier it is to find the correct scale fingering. For example, if I start on the same Bb with my fourth finger, it ends up being part of the same pattern we just played, but three frets lower.

Example 1i

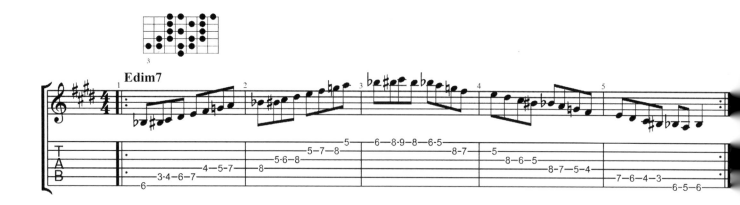

Before we move on, let's play the position-based pattern moving up the neck in minor 3rds. You'll ascend one pattern, then shift up to the next pattern to descend, and so on.

Example 1j

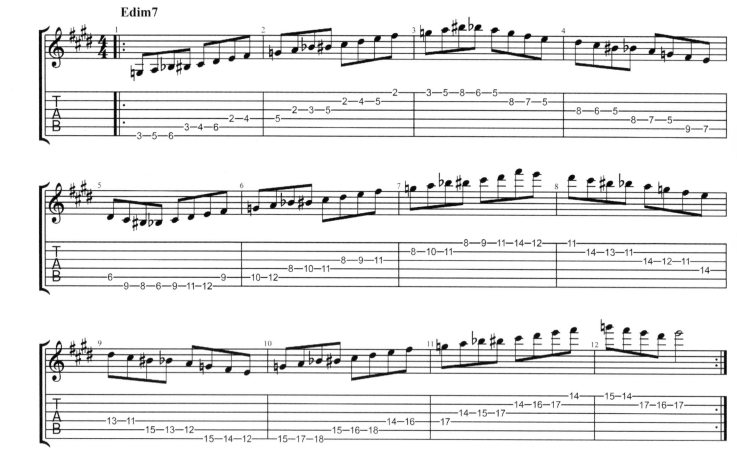

We've spent some time looking at different ways to play this scale, but the question is: *why* play this scale? What exactly is the Whole-Half Diminished scale for?

The answer is that it fits perfectly over a diminished 7 chord.

Just as we'd use the C Major scale (C, D, E, F, G, A, B, C) if we wanted to play over a Cmaj7 chord because it contains every note, we'd use the C Whole-Half Diminished scale if we wanted to play over a Cdim7.

The C Whole-Half Diminished scale contains the notes:

C – D – Eb – F – Gb – G# – A – B

And Cdim7 contains the notes C, Eb, Gb and A.

Let me quickly point out something about note naming in the diminished scale. As soon as we create an eight-note scale, one letter has to appear twice. I opted for Gb and G#, so that the next note in the scale is an A. Some readers will be aware that, technically, the spelling of Cdim7 should be C, Eb, Gb, Bbb (B double flat), but this approach can look messy in notation.

Moving on, it's really important to visualise the scale pattern around diminished chord voicings to strengthen the chord-scale connection in your mind.

Here's a Cdim7 chord with its root note on the fifth string, and the C Whole-Half Diminished scale played ascending from the root.

Example 1k

The previous scale pattern extended across the strings a little. Here's the same voicing of Cdim7 but with a scale fingering that remains in position.

Example 1l

Just as we can move Whole-Half Diminished scale patterns around in minor 3rds, we can do the same with diminished 7 chord voicings. If we move the Cdim7 voicing up three frets we get Ebdim7, which can be thought of as an inversion of Cdim7 with Eb as the lowest note.

Paired with this voicing is a new scale pattern that is used less frequently, but is still worth knowing. It also has an alternating fingering pattern but spans more frets.

Example 1m

If we move the previous chord voicing up another three frets we get a Cdim7 with a Gb in the bass (a.k.a. Gbdim7). Playing C Whole-Half Diminished from the root note on the fourth string, 10th fret, gives us this pattern.

Example 1n

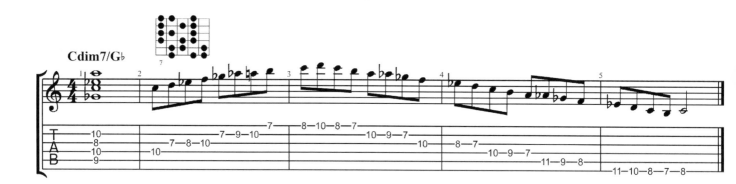

Moving the voicing up one final time gives us Cdim7 with an A (technically Bbb) in the bass, and we can flesh out the scale as follows.

Example 1o

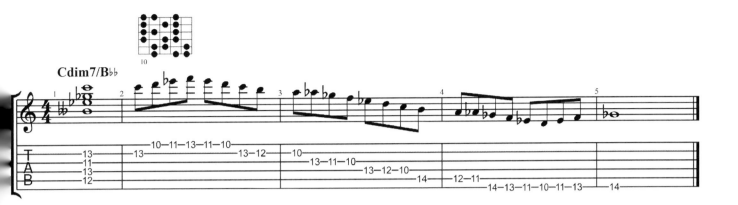

Now let's look at a couple of split-voiced diminished 7 chords that have a root note on the sixth string and skip the fifth string.

This time we're going to play the chord, then ascend the Whole-Half Diminished scale starting from the lowest chord tone. Then we'll shift up three frets and ascend the scale from the second note in the chord, then shift up again and play it from the third note, and finally shift to play it from the fourth note.

Example 1p

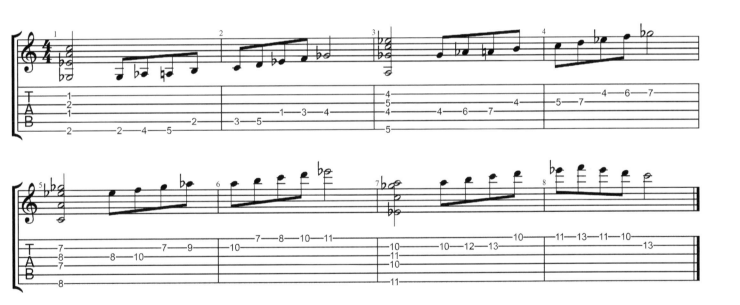

Let's do something similar based on a common diminished chord voicing on the top four strings. This time we're going to play the chord and immediately descend the scale, as though we're using the chord to punctuate a melody.

Example 1q

We'll finish this chapter with a few short musical examples that use this scale.

First, we have to find a chord progression that includes a diminished chord. One that always springs to mind for me is a jazz blues, and the movement from the IV chord back to the I.

Example 1r

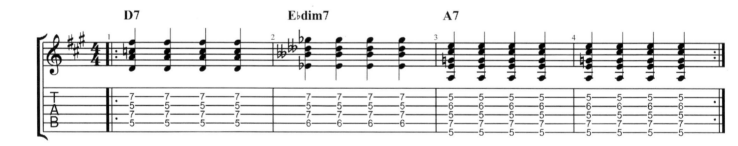

The first lick we're going to play begins with a simple triad-based melody over the D7 chord, then uses the ascending Eb Whole-Half Diminished scale over the Ebdim7 chord. It ends with a descending A7 melody.

Example 1s

The next lick features a few more notes, this time starting with a 3rd to 9th arpeggio over the D7 before linking to a straight Whole-Half Diminished scale over the Ebdim7, then another strong melody over the A7.

Example 1t

The final lick shifts up the neck with a triplet, connecting to an ascending Whole-Half Diminished scale over Ebdim7 and ending with an A7 melody that includes a chromatic walkdown from the A root to G (b7).

Example 1u

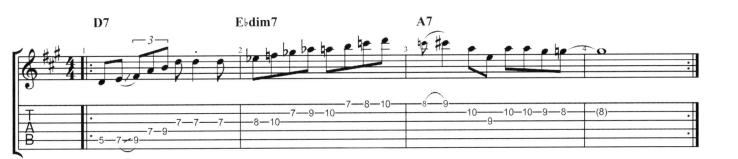

So far, we've learned that we can play the Whole-Half Diminished scale whenever we see a diminished chord, which is pretty straightforward. But it's worth noting one other chord voicing you'll sometimes see, which is harder to spot as originating from the diminished 7 chord.

Our Cdim7 chord was formed with the notes C, Eb, Gb, A (Bbb). It's possible to use the diminished triad and add a B note on top instead, so that we have C, Eb, Gb, B.

I've seen this chord called a "diminished major" because it's a diminished triad with an added major 7th.

We can make this sound by taking any diminished 7 chord voicings and moving up *any* of the notes a whole step. The following example shows how this is commonly done.

Example 1v

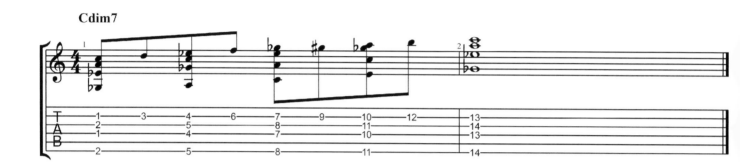

That's it for the Whole-Half Diminished scale. Now let's move on and flip it on its head!

Chapter Two – Half-Whole Diminished Scale

We've spent some time getting to grips with the Whole-Half Diminished scale and now we're going to look at its Half-Whole counterpart.

You might wonder why we need the complication of another version of the diminished scale. Can't we just skip it and use one diminished scale for all purposes?

First, it's useful to understand that the Half-Whole Diminished scale is really a mode of the Whole-Half scale. Because the diminished scale is symmetrical, it has just two modes: one that begins with a whole step interval and one that begins with a half step.

The Whole-Half Diminished scale follows the pattern:

W – H – W – H – W – H – W – H – W – H etc.

If we skip the first note and play that pattern from the second step, we get:

H – W – H – W – H – W – H – W – H – W etc.

Both scales use the same pattern, just starting from different points.

Second, players such as Robben Ford and Mike Stern think about the diminished scale from a Half-Whole perspective and use it to play over dominant 7 chords, so in this chapter we'll look at why and how that works.

We'll use the C Half-Whole Diminished scale as our workhorse. Here's the scale played from a sixth string root note.

Example 2a

The C Half-Whole scale has these notes:

C – Db – Eb – E – F# – G – A – Bb

In intervals, that can be expressed as:

R – b2 – #2/b3 – 3 – #4/b5 – 5 – 6 – b7

We can find a lot of chords in that set of intervals. There's a dominant 7 (root, 3rd, 5th, b7), a minor 7 (root, b3, 5th, b7) and a minor 7b5 (root, b3, b5, b7), as well as the diminished 7 (root, b3, b5, bb7 – the 6th is the same note as the bb7 interval).

Where the Half-Whole really comes into its own is that it also contains the notes needs to build altered dominant chords. We can make a dominant 7b9, 7#9, 7#11 and even a 13b9. The only alteration the scale doesn't have is the #5 interval.

Before we go any further, I want to give the Half-Whole Diminished scale a new name. Why? Because we need to understand this scale in terms of *how* it is used. For that reason, it's commonly referred to as the *Dominant Diminished* scale.

That's how I prefer to file it in my brain and is how I refer to it when teaching. From now on, let's think of our two scales as the Diminished scale (Whole-Half) mainly used over diminished 7 chords, and the Dominant Diminished scale (Half-Whole) mainly used over dominant 7 chords.

Let's hear how the C Dominant Diminished scale sounds against a straight C7 chord.

Example 2b

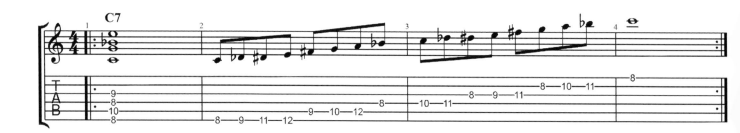

If you've studied my guided practice books, you'll know that the aim with any scale is to be able to play it around *any* voicing of the chord it fits. So, the first goal is to learn this scale around any dominant 7 chord voicing.

I'll only demonstrate one more example for you here, but in your practice time work out the other C7 chord voicings across the fretboard and practice the scale from the root of each one. This example shows the scale built around a C7 chord using the CAGED system A shape.

Example 2c

Although we can play C Dominant Diminished over a plain C7 chord (and it will sound like we're playing outside-inside type lines) it's ideal to use over altered dominant chords, because it contains every dominant 7 chord tone and three of the four possible altered tone options.

In other words, we can play Dominant Diminished lines over chords that contain different combinations of the b9, #9, b5 and 6th/13th (but remember the scale does not have the #5, so it doesn't work as well on chords containing that interval).

Here is a selection of C7alt chords that the C Dominant Diminished scale works over.

Example 2d

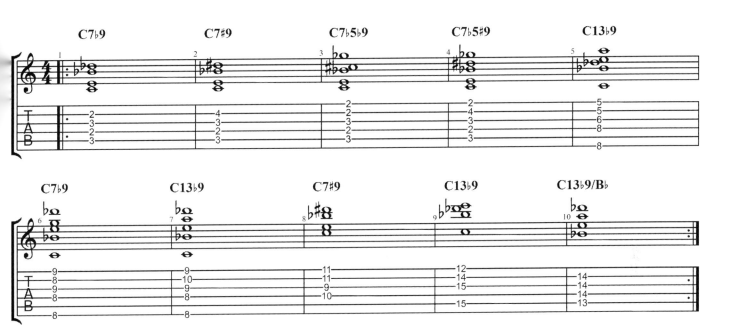

To my ears, the 13b9 is the chord that most encapsulates the Dominant Diminished sound. The 7b9 is close too, but that chord can also be found in the Altered and Phrygian Dominant scales. The 13b9 is uniquely diminished. You might notice that the last voicing above doesn't even contain the root note. That's OK, that's the bass player's job!

Let's use the 13b9 chord sound in a progression, so we have a reason to include the Dominant Diminished sound in our practice.

In a blues in C, chord IV is F7 (in bar five). In bar four, we'll use the 13b9 sound to create some tension that will resolve to the F7 chord. Here's how that sounds.

Example 2e

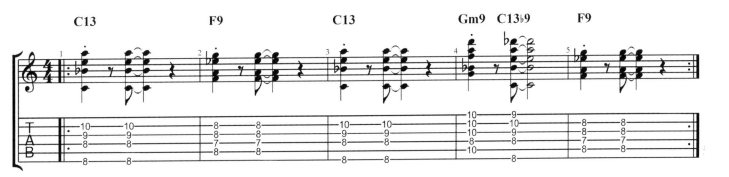

The easiest way to get this scale happening in your playing is to start by inserting it, ascending or descending, over the altered dominant chord it fits over. Here's an example where we play some melodic ideas over the other chords, then connect them to an ascending C Dominant Diminished scale over C13b9.

Example 2f

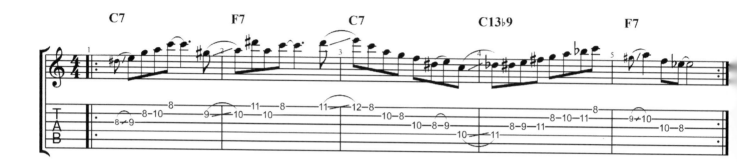

Let's do that again but using a different melodic idea.

Example 2g

Here's another, but now descending the scale on the 13b9 chord.

Example 2h

Finally, a faster descending triplet run leading to the F7 chord. I like this sound because it feels like we're rushing down a waterslide to our destination!

Example 2i

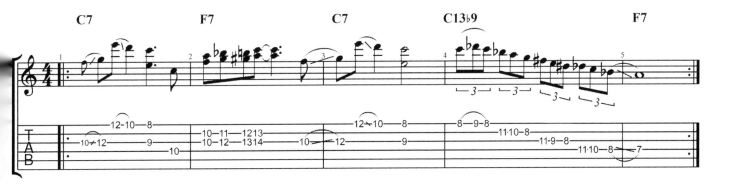

Now you've got the sound of the scale in your ears, I want to show you a quick hack for visualising it on the fretboard.

Look at the C7b9 chord below. Take away the root note and you'll see a diminished chord shape sitting on the top four strings.

C7b9 is really a Dbdim7 chord played on top of a C root note. We can call this chord C7b9 or Dbdim7/C and it's the same thing. We can also call it Edim7/C, Gdim7/C or Bbdim7/C. The symmetrical nature of the scale means that we can move diminished chords around in minor 3rds and they'll all be inversions of each other.

Example 2j

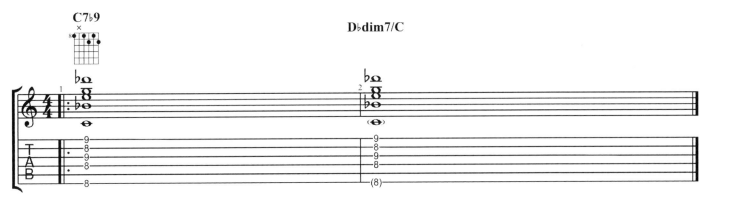

Jazz musicians have called this the "dominant-diminished connection" and it's the idea behind chord progressions where you see diminished chords being played in place of dominant chords. Let's explore this idea a little.

Here's a I VI7 ii V7 progression in the key of C Major. That's C – A7 – Dm7 – G7.

Example 2k

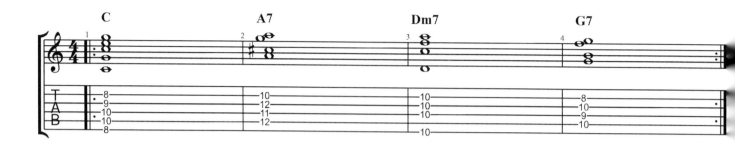

We can make this progression more interesting by turning the plain A7 chord into an A7b9. How do we do this? In the previous example we visualised a diminished chord shape sitting on top of a C root note. This gave us four possible diminished chords we could play.

We can do the same thing over an A root note. In fact, we can play *any* of the *same* four chords as before, because the dominant chords in question (C7 and A7) are a minor 3rd interval apart.

Here's the same progression played twice. The first time around we play a Gdim7 in place of the A7 chord. That's a diminished chord played from the b7 of the A7 chord.

The second time we play C#dim7. That's a diminished chord played from the 3rd of A7.

Can you see the dominant-diminished connection? Equally, we could have played an Edim7 or Bbdim7 chord in place of the A7.

Example 2l

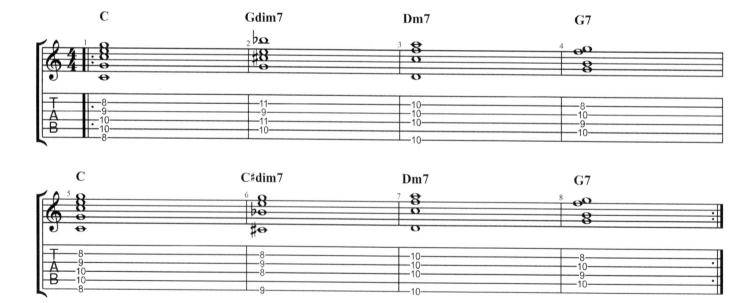

We can do the same thing with the G7 chord. Play a G7b9 with its root on the sixth string, 3rd fret, and you can visualise an Abdim7 sitting on top of the G root. This means that Abdim7, Bdim7, Ddim7 and Fdim7 are all options to play instead of G7. All we've done is taken that Abdim7 shape and moved it up three-fret intervals.

In this example, let's play two diminished chords in the A7 and G7 bars.

In bar two, we're playing Gdim7 then moving down a minor 3rd to play Edim7 in place of the A7 chord. In bar six, we're playing C#dim7 then Edim7 in place of the A7.

Similarly, in bar four we have Fdim7 and Ddim7 in place of G7, and Bdim7 and Ddim7 in bar eight.

Example 2m

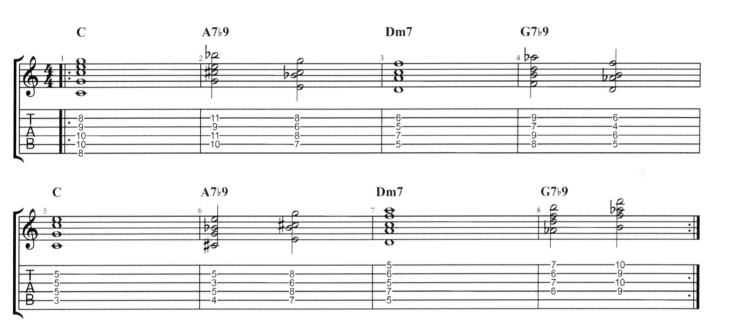

Now let's apply this idea in a soloing context.

We're going to play over the progression A7 – D7, with two bars of each chord. For the first bar of A7 we'll use blues, pentatonic and mixolydian sounds, then for the second bar we'll use the diminished sound.

All these licks were improvised off the cuff. I played them as I would in a live situation, rather than sitting down to compose them. To get the dominant diminished sound, I was looking for the 3rd, 5th, b7 or b9 intervals of A7, then playing the A Dominant Diminished scale from that note. That's me visualising the diminished chord. Then, of course, we have to resolve the melodic idea to the D7 chord that follows!

To begin with, here's a lick around the A shape of the A7 chord. In bar two, I locate the b9 of A7 (Bb) and use it as a springboard for my diminished line.

Example 2n

The next lick starts in the same place and begins the diminished scale from the same note, but this time the diminished scale moves up.

Example 2o

Here's one more lick in that position, now with a longer scale pattern.

Example 2p

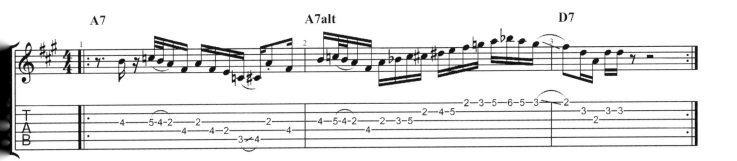

Now we move up to the E shape of A7, but the concept is the same. We go from an A Mixolydian idea to A Dominant Diminished (finding it from the b9) and resolve to D7.

Example 2q

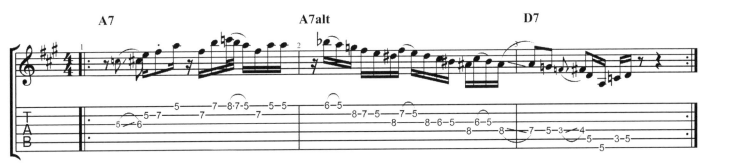

Here's one final idea starting in the E shape.

Example 2r

Integrating the sound of this scale into your playing may take some time, but hopefully you're starting to get it in your ear.

That's it for the theory! From here on, we're going to spend several chapters exploring interesting methods of practicing and bringing out the sound of the diminished scale. Don't be afraid to take a break and go back over chapters one and two. We're going to work on more applications at the end of the book, so having a firm knowledge of *why* we're applying the scales in this way will help!

Chapter Three – Sequence Practice

If you've read my Guided Practice Routines for Guitar series of books, you'll know I'm a firm believer in the use of sequences to develop fretboard knowledge.

To me, a scale is like an alphabet – it's a nice, organised way of learning all the letters in a language. When we speak, of course we want to use words, phrases and sentences, not just recite the alphabet – but that doesn't mean that scalar ideas in music are useless; we just don't want them to be the *only* expression of our melodic ideas.

I'm of the opinion that if you practice scales in an up and down, linear way, that's how you'll play them when improvising. So, it's important to practice scales in a non-linear fashion, to push your scalic ideas into melodic territory. If you do that, then you've moved beyond treating the scale as an alphabet – you're using actual words and phrases.

How do we define a "sequence"? It's simply a pattern where two or more elements are arranged in successive order. Here is a typical sequence:

1234 2345 3456 4567

Because the numbers are organised into a sequence, we can work out that the next group of numbers will be 5678 and not 1538! We're creating an ascending sequence in groups of four.

We apply this sequence to the diminished scale. Here's the C Whole-Half Diminished scale played in a sequence of ascending fours over a Cdim7 chord.

Example 3a

We could play this sequence in a different position in order to get a little more range, with the pattern starting on the sixth string root played with the fourth finger.

Example 3b

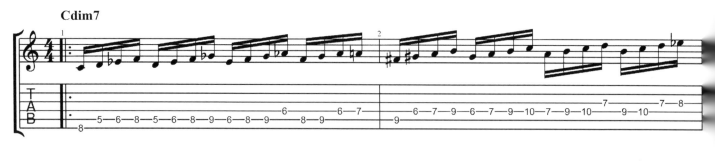

Or we could arrange it with the root note on the sixth string played with the first finger. Organising it this way results in a trickier stretch between the fifth and fourth strings, so it's worth practicing.

Example 3c

Once you're worked on this sequence ascending, it makes sense to be able to do it descending too.

Example 3d

Again, there are alternate ways to finger the pattern. Here's a different approach to descending.

Example 3e

When you've practiced this pattern and are able to play it without much thought, the next logical step is to work on connecting ascending and descending runs of fours. You could finger this idea in a ton of different ways, but here's a good starting point.

Example 3f

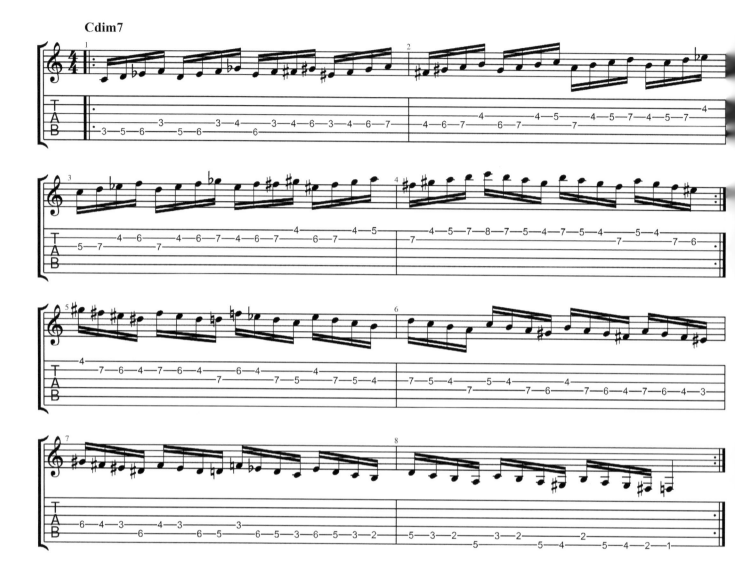

Another sequence we can use is:

3123 4234 5345 6456 etc.

Applied to our diminished scale, it gives us this pattern.

Example 3g

Here's that sequence played descending. One of the things that makes these sequences so cool is that they give the listener something they can predict. It's easy to hear the first eight notes then know where the melody is going next.

Example 3h

The previous idea introduced some melodic leaps in minor 3rds. We could expand on this by playing a sequence of just diatonic 3rds. I.e.:

13 24 35 46 57 68, and so on.

When played on the guitar in an ascending fashion, it looks and sounds like this.

Example 3i

Here's the same idea, but with a little more range.

Example 3j

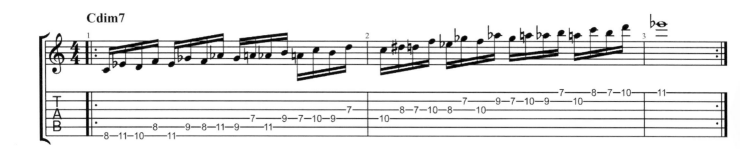

As you might expect, you can also play these patterns in a descending fashion.

Example 3k

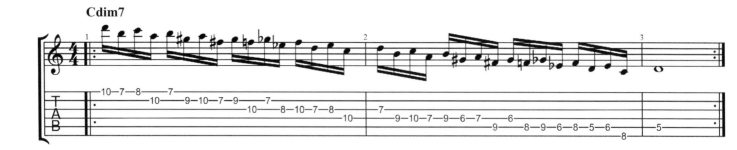

Then you can combine those ascending and descending ideas into a longer exercise.

Example 3l

So far, these sequences have been relatively simple, but the nature of sequences is that they can be as complicated as you want them to be. The one problem we face is that the nature of the guitar is such that some sequences present significant technical challenges, which an instrument like the saxophone doesn't experience.

I accept this and lean towards doing things that lend themselves to the guitar. But we could take something like a 6th interval and use it to harmonise the diminished scale. This is hard!

Example 3m

We're going to revisit the idea of playing sequences later on, where we'll draw inspiration from the playing style of some great horn players, but at this stage, it's fine to stick with more guitaristic patterns. Take your time exploring these all over the neck before you move on.

Chapter Four – Diminished Arpeggios

I put a lot of value on moving away from linear approaches towards melody. There's nothing wrong with using a scalic approach, but being versatile enough to remove the predictability of ascending and descending scales is more exciting. So, in this chapter we'll begin to look at how we can use arpeggios from the diminished scale for a more melodic approach.

Let's look at the notes of the C Whole-Half Diminished scale:

C D Eb F Gb G# A B C

We can derive a lot of chords/arpeggios from that collection of notes:

- Cdim, Cdim7

- Dm, Dmin7, Dm7b5, Ddim, Ddim7, D major

- Ebdim

- Fm, Fm7, F7, F major

- Gbdim

- Abm, Abm7, Abdim, Abdim7, Ab7, Ab major

- Bm, Bm7, Bdim, Bdim7, B7, B major

Even that is not comprehensive! There are a *lot* of chords that can be found in an eight-note scale.

When thinking about what we can do with those arpeggios, the best place to start is with the scale's namesake – the diminished 7 arpeggio – played from the root of the scale. That means we can play Cdim7 arpeggios over Cdim7 chords. But remember we can also play them over B7b9 chords (that's our Dominant Diminished scale! Visualise the Cdim7 chord on the top four strings sitting on top of a B bass note).

Just like the diminished scale patterns we've looked at, diminished arpeggios give us the same symmetrical benefits/challenges. Because they function as a series of repeating minor 3rd intervals we have a lot of options for playing them.

However, the most common way you'll see a diminished arpeggio played is across the strings, like this, ascending and descending.

Example 4a

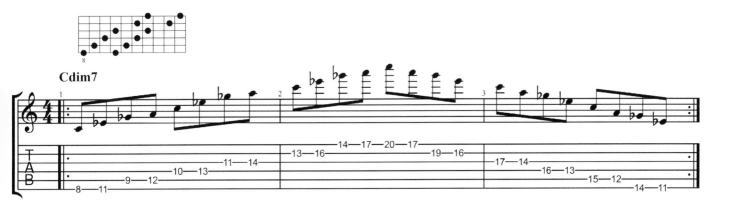

This common two-note-per-string pattern will allow you to dip your toe into the water of diminished arpeggios, but real mastery of the diminished arpeggio comes from being able to freely integrate single notes on strings. That idea creates this common pattern, which as you can see, moves up the neck three frets at a time.

Example 4b

You can work on this idea by always starting the arpeggio on the third string and ascending.

Example 4c

This pattern is popular among neo-classical shredders like Yngwie Malmsteen, where you'll find licks like this sweep picking pattern.

Example 4d

Many rock players stop at the previous pattern, but we can move it over a string set and end up with the following idea. We're starting on a Gb here, which still makes the Cdim7 sound, because Cdim7 has the same notes as Gbdim7, Adim7 and Ebdim7!

This time we're playing groups of five notes on each beat, which allows us to keep the first note of each arpeggio on the beat.

Example 4e

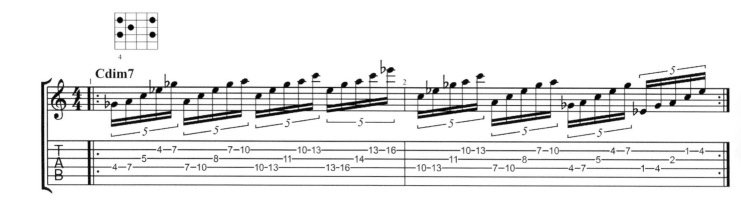

I love combining these patterns like this.

Example 4f

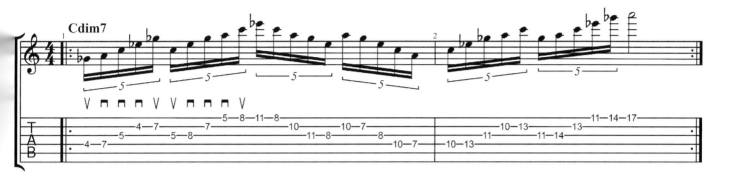

This three-string pattern can be moved over to the lower string sets, where it's a little harder to play but looks like this.

Example 4g

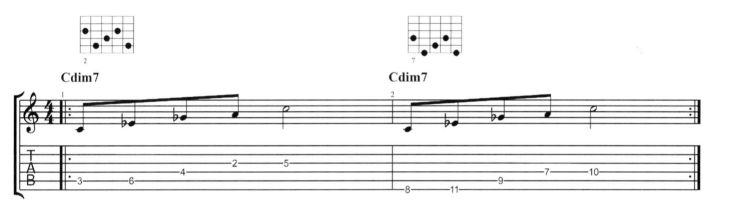

We could combine those five-note groupings to get a nice little picking workout like this.

Example 4h

Knowing these patterns will enable you to play in position more effectively, and this will make it easier to blend in scale ideas. It's a good discipline to have, to be able to start on a given root note and play a full arpeggio while remaining in position. Starting on the sixth string, you might do it like this.

Example 4i

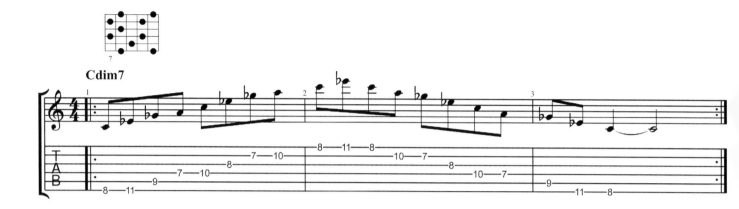

But you can also choose to do it like this.

Example 4j

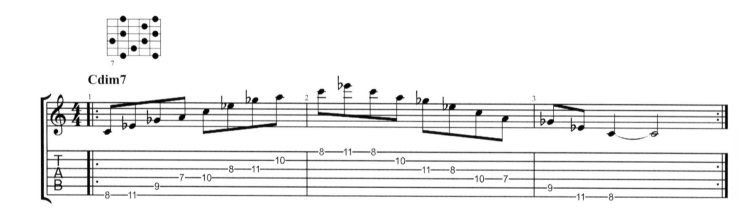

Or even like this.

Example 4k

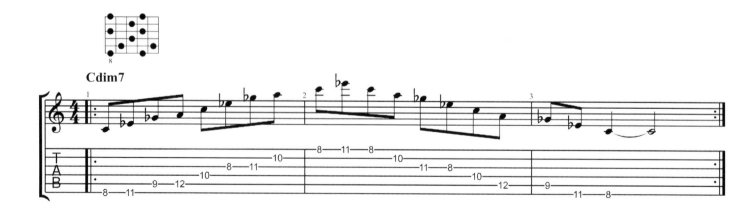

If we move this idea over and play it from a root note on the fifth string, we have just as many options. We can play it like this.

Example 4l

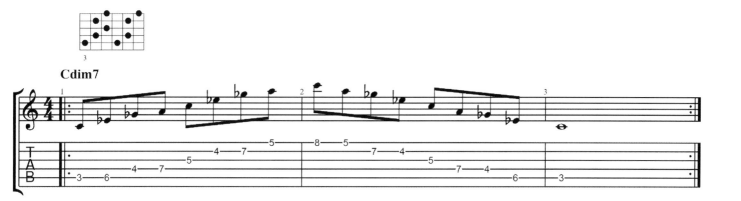

And here's another option.

Example 4m

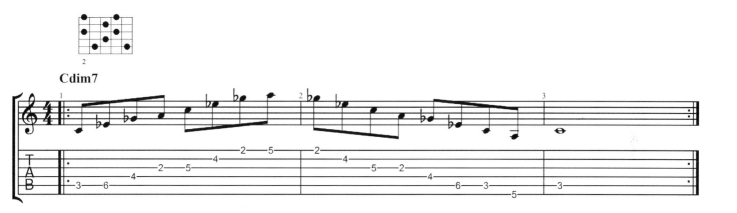

Before combining this idea with scales, it makes sense to see if we can use these arpeggios over an actual chord progression to create the sound we want.

Let's go back to the progression we used in Chapter Two: C – A7 – Dm7 – G7.

Remember that if we want to imply a dominant 7b9 sound, we can play a diminished arpeggio from the 3rd, 5th, b7 or b9 of the chord.

Here's one way of achieving that. Over the C7 chord we're using the C Major Pentatonic scale, then connecting it to a C#dim7 arpeggio over A7 to make A7b9. We play a Dm7 arpeggio over the Dm7 chord in bar three, then use an Abdim7 over the G7 in bar four to make G7b9.

Example 4n

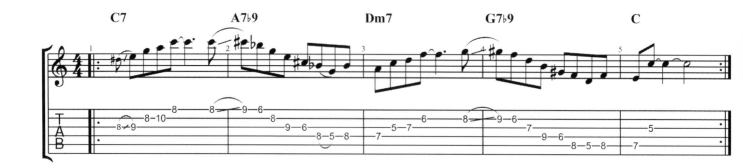

Here's another example using the same approach. We could make 1,000 licks like this and each time we are just looking for the right diminished arpeggio to connect our ideas.

Example 4o

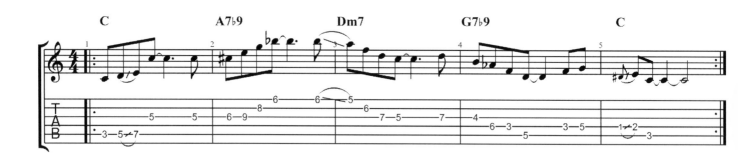

Now let's look at integrating the diminished scale *around* our diminished arpeggio.

We're drawing our ideas from the Whole-Half Diminished scale. That means for any note in the arpeggio there is a scale tone located a half step *below* the arpeggio tone or a whole step *above*.

For example, if we want to play a diminished 7 arpeggio then transition into the scale, we can find it by moving a half step below any note in the arpeggio then fill in the scale from there.

Here's that idea applied to the top three strings, then moved up three frets to take advantage of the symmetrical nature of the scale/arpeggio.

Example 4p

We could play that example a little differently by adding another note from the diminished arpeggio.

Example 4q

You can extend this sort of idea by connecting an arpeggio to the scale, then moving back to the arpeggio, then ending with the scale.

Example 4r

Now I want to flip this idea on its head by ascending a scale, then descending an arpeggio. This time I'm applying the idea to the fourth, third and second strings.

Remember, it's the higher of the two notes a half step apart that are in our diminished arpeggio.

Example 4s

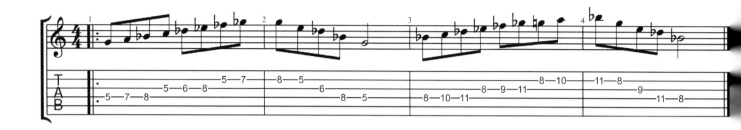

You can make these ideas longer too, as shown in this idea which mixes ascending and descending scales with small arpeggio fragments.

Example 4t

And to finish up, here's an idea you could use in a more rock or fusion setting, but you'll need the technique to match it!

Example 4u

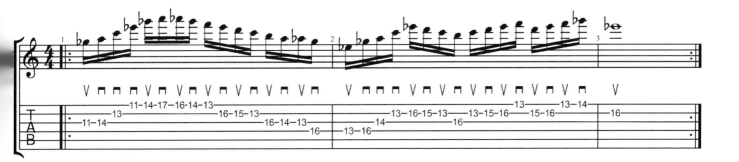

We're going to revisit arpeggios later, but in the meantime, know that just using diminished arpeggios as part of your diminished playing is a very effective approach. Have some fun with it!

Chapter Five – Pattern Based Playing

So far, everything we've covered in this book has involved taking a musical concept and applying it to the guitar. We've looked at scales, sequences and arpeggios, then worked out how to apply them to our instrument. We've followed a theory-led approach, and there's nothing wrong with that. In fact, the challenges involved in this approach force us to get to grips with fretboard navigation, and that's good.

But, at the same time, we recognise that the guitar is a beautiful instrument because, while it can be approached in a theory-led manner, we can also ignore all of that! We can simply discover physical patterns on the fretboard that we find easy to memorise or just like the sound of.

Many blues and rock players take the latter approach. The question, "Why do these notes work?" can only really be answered with, "Because I like the way they sound."

In academic circles, this approach is often looked down on, but it shouldn't be. The only thing that matters in music is *the music* i.e., the way it sounds, not how well it can be explained. I like to say:

If the music sounds good to you, no explanation is needed. If it doesn't, then no explanation will help.

So, as a change from our theory-led approach, in this chapter we're going to take the diminished patterns we've learned and apply a "shape-based approach" to creating melodic content.

As a reminder, here is our C Whole-Half Diminished scale pattern:

Example 5a

Played from the sixth string root, the scale has a repeating fingering pattern of 1 3 4, 1 2 4 on each pair of strings. Example 5b shows that a little more clearly. Each string pair doesn't contain the same notes, but does follow the same physical pattern.

Example 5b

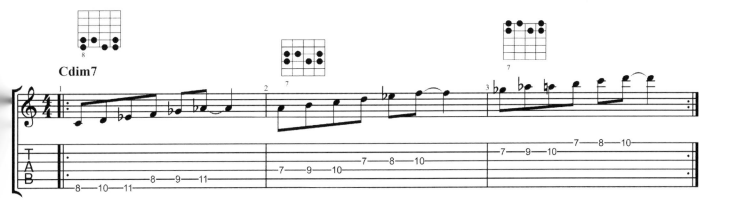

Because of the symmetrical nature of the scale, we can repeat these ideas every three frets.

Example 5c

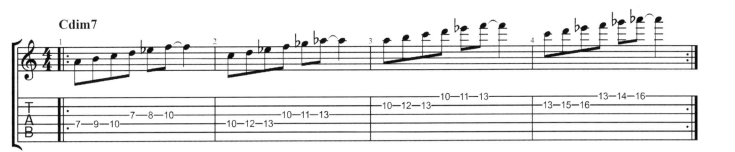

In fact, we can take any selection of notes from the scale, apply a pattern, and move it up or down in minor 3rd (three fret) intervals. For example:

Example 5d

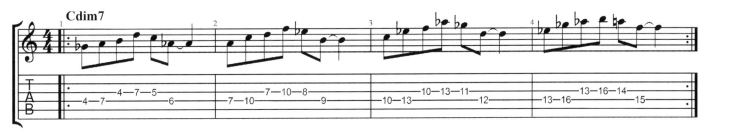

Now, let's play the exact same shape, but move it across the strings instead of along them. In this example, after doing that four times, we end by descending the scale.

It doesn't matter how you order the notes in these patterns, you can just take something and move it around.

Example 5e

One of my favourite things to do is to pair up notes from the scale on adjacent strings. Here's that idea shown as double-stops.

Example 5f

When played as a melodic exercise, we get something that sounds pretty cool.

Example 5g

But it gets even cooler if we start changing the direction of some of the intervals and continuing the pattern down the neck.

Example 5h

Or we can take part of that pattern and move it down in three fret jumps, like this.

Example 5i

As you can hear, ideas like this sound just as cool when we're ascending too.

Example 5j

There really are no limits when it comes to shape-based playing using the diminished scale. Here's anothe[?] little fragment that feels really nice to move across the strings. When coming up with this, I didn't start with [?] theoretical concept, it was just something that felt easy for my fingers.

Example 5k

The magic of an idea like this is that it's a seven-note phrase. We can play it like we did in the previous example, with each motif starting in a new bar, or we can just stitch it all together so that we end up with something a little more jarring.

Example 5l

Now we move on to what I think of as "pentatonic" patterns. They aren't really pentatonic at all, because we're using an eight-note, not a five-note scale, but we can apply *pentatonic-style* fingering and phrasing, arranging the scale in two-note-per-string patterns which are easy to play.

Example 5m shows a diminished scale pattern arranged on the top four strings in bars 1-2. Bars 3-4 show how we can turn that into a two-note-per-string pattern.

Example 5m

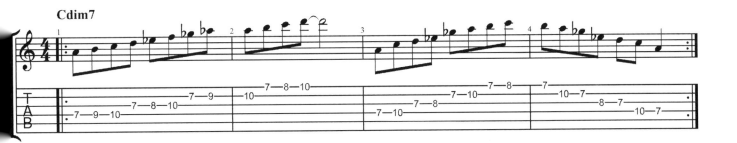

If I apply some chops to that pattern, we might end up with something like this.

Example 5n

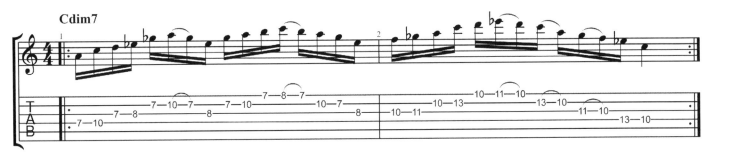

Here's another lick that draws from those two-note-per-string ideas, but this time we're connecting it to the scale, descending in 3rds.

Example 5o

I love this approach to playing diminished scale lines. They're very *guitary,* but then I'm a guitarist! I love that sound and it fits nicely under the fingers.

Here's another lick, but with more position shifts.

Example 5p

We can extend the two-note-per-string idea across all six strings.

Example 5q

Once again, I can easily turn that into something that sounds a little wilder by applying patterns I might apply to the minor pentatonic scale.

Example 5r

Or I might play something like this.

Example 5s

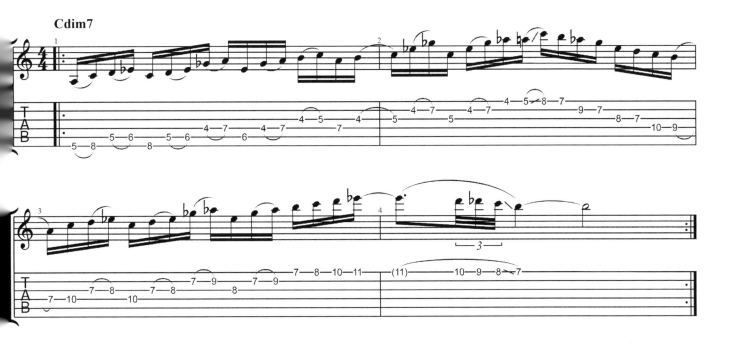

To end this chapter, I want to revisit the A7 – D7 chord progression we worked with at the end of Chapter Two, and play some real-world examples that show how I would use these patterns when improvising.

These are all examples of diminished phrasing over the A7alt chord, but there's lots of cool A7 and D7 lines to steal too!

First up is a lick that begins in the E shape of A7.

Example 5t

In this lick, we have a similar diminished lick, but phrased three frets higher.

Example 5u

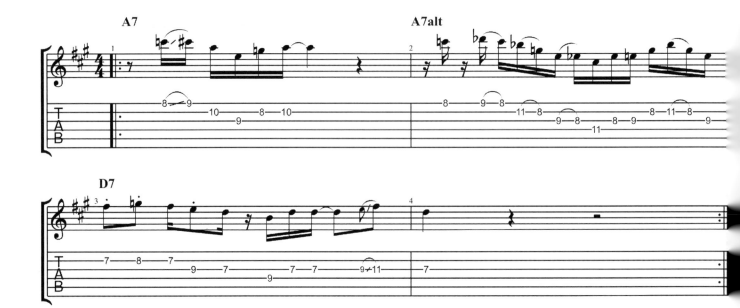

Now I'm combining two ascending ideas across the fourth, third and second strings, moving up three frets, then resolving to the D7 chord.

Example 5v

Here's another idea, starting a little higher on the neck.

Example 5w

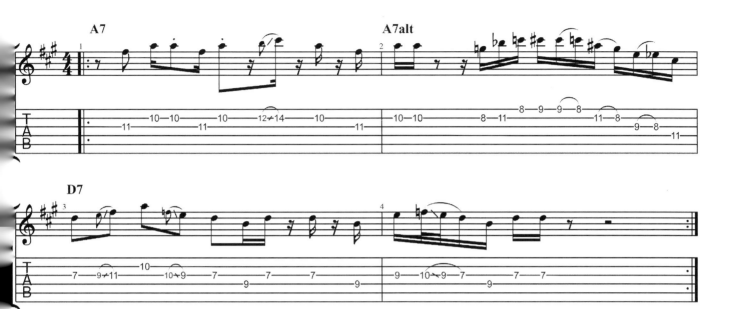

There are limitless options here and I'd urge you to spend hours playing around with these ideas over backing tracks, until you really start integrating them in your own lines. You'll feel like John Scofield or Scott Henderson in no time at all!

Chapter Six – Common Jazz Sequences

I've been fascinated by the sound of the diminished scale since I was a teenager. Back then, when I started getting into jazz and listening to the great saxophonists, I picked up all manner of educational materials and slammed my head against the wall for hours on end, trying to nail the sequences the great horn players encouraged their students to work on.

But, as we've discussed, there are some things that the guitar does really well and other things that feel so much harder. In this chapter we're going to look at some ideas commonly used in modern jazz, and we'll tackle them in two ways:

First, we'll embrace the nature of the guitar, which will mean changing positions a lot. These ideas will often be easy to visualise but tricky to pull off, due to those position shifts.

Second, we'll learn to play the same ideas while remaining in position. This is going to be a world harder, as it will often feel impossible to *see* the sequence on the fretboard, despite being able to hear it quite clearly.

Eventually, I had my suspicions confirmed by a great sax playing friend of mine. There is no trick to playing these sequences on other instruments – those who have mastered them have simply put in the hours and developed the appropriate muscle memory.

For the guitar player, our struggle appears to be accepting that there are exponentially more ways to finger a sequence than a saxophonist or pianist has to deal with. But we can mitigate this by finding one fingering and sticking to it until it becomes second nature.

The first common jazz sequence is a "targeting" idea called an enclosure. The idea is to target the notes of a Cdim7 arpeggio by playing a note above, a note below, and then the target note.

For example, to target the A note we'll play B (a whole step above), G# (half step below) then A (the target note).

Next, we'll target the C note, so we'll play D (whole step above), B (half step below) then C, etc.

We can lay this out easily on the guitar by playing all three notes of the sequence on the same string, then moving the three-note motif around. Here's that being done with a longer rhythm on the target note.

Example 6a

Playing sequences with uneven rhythms is a great way to focus on embedding the motif you're working with. You can translate it into a more consistent rhythm once you're comfortable, like this.

Example 6b

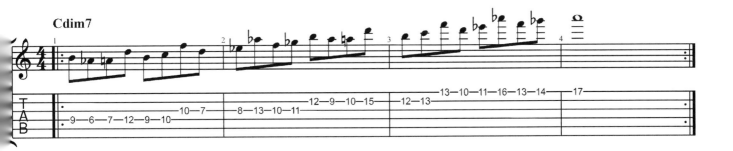

Now we're going to play the same sequence, but this time keep it in position. This is infinitely harder as we need to deal with several different finger patterns. It can be confusing at first, but if we stick with it long enough it'll get embedded into our muscle memory – it just takes time.

Example 6c

Descending that pattern looks like this when played the easy way.

Example 6d

Which means that we could connect the ascending and descending patterns like this.

Example 6e

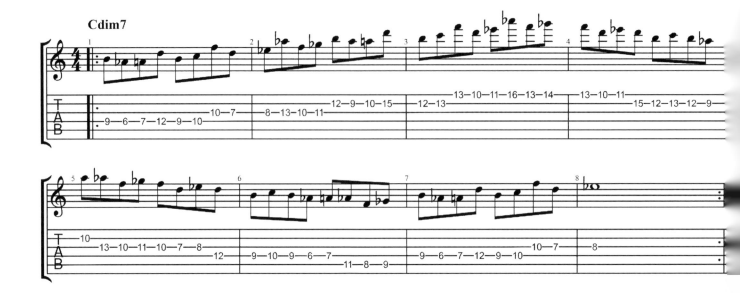

Now for the nightmare of playing the same kind of ascending and descending idea across the strings. Take your time with this one!

Example 6f

Next up, we're going to look at an ascending sequence based on the notes of a Cdim7 chord (C, Eb, Gb, A). The pattern is to play a chord tone, ascend a scale tone, ascend a major 3rd, then ascend another scale tone.

So, we begin on the C root, move up a scale tone to D, move up a 3rd to F#, then move up another scale tone to G#.

Next, we move to the Eb, up a whole step to F, up a 3rd to A, and up a whole step to B, etc.

If we apply that to the guitar using our shifting pattern, we get Example 6g. Once again, we'll start by giving each motif a bit more space in the bar, so you can really learn the pattern.

Example 6g

Here it is without the gaps. The third to second string pattern is a little tricky!

Example 6h

When played across the strings, we end up with a real finger twister that looks like this.

Example 6i

Remember, you can play this pattern starting on any of the notes in the diminished 7 chord, or just move it up or down in three-fret intervals!

Example 6j

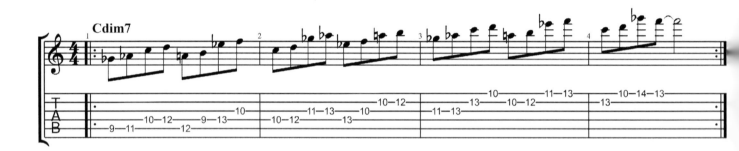

I love playing this one in a descending fashion. It's something I remember learning from the great Don Mock many moons ago!

Example 6k

Let's place a section of that sequence in the middle of a diminished phrase that combines scale patterns, the two-note-per-string approach, and the sequence. Remember that while we're learning patterns, we don't want our playing to *sound* like we're running patterns! Combining everything we know will sound the most musical.

Example 6l

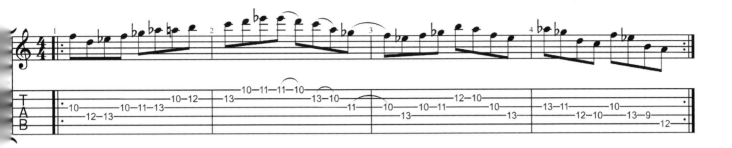

Another sequence I've seen horn players practice is beginning on the root, ascending a whole step, jumping up a tritone (b5) then descending a whole step.

For example, from the Eb chord tone we move up a whole step to F, jump up to B (the b5), then move down a whole step to A.

Here's that applied to the neck using guitar friendly patterns.

Example 6m

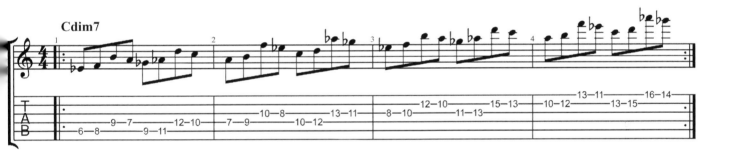

Now here is the trickier way of playing it. Notice the string skip between the third and first strings. This is inevitable when we introduce wider intervals like the b5.

Example 6n

Now we need to take a look at that in the descending direction.

Example 6o

The sky is the limit with this stuff. If you want to go angular, you can do that. Maybe you take a note, go up a 6th, then up a whole step, then down a 4th. This is what that looks like this as a pattern.

Example 6p

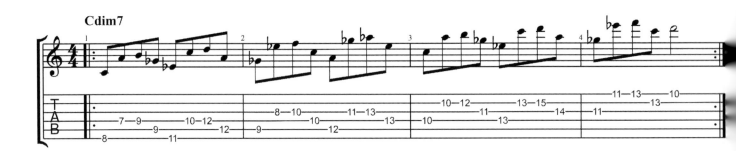

We end up with a real workout when trying to keep that in position.

Example 6q

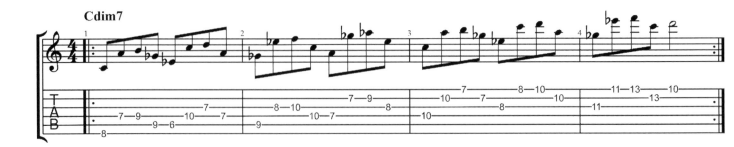

Let's finish by extending the simple 3rds idea we looked at earlier. As a reminder, here's that sequence, which plays a note from the scale, skips a note, plays another scale note, then jumps back to the note we missed to repeat the pattern, and so on.

Example 6r

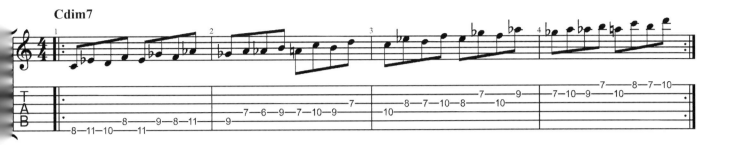

A more advanced take on that might be to extend the pattern by playing a note, skipping a note, playing a note, skipping a note, and playing a note. That gives us a three-note motif we can move through the diminished scale. These all end up being diminished triads, so it helps if you know them well!

Example 6s

We'll go out of our way to use more of these ideas later when we look at musical context, but in the meantime keep practicing them ascending and descending. And remember, the nature of the diminished scale dictates that these licks repeat in three-fret intervals.

Get to work!

Chapter Seven – Triad Pairs

Now we move onto one of the most exciting concepts in this book – combining triad pairs to express th diminished sound.

I've purposely waited until now to point out something you may have missed – that the diminished scale itself is just a pair of interlocking diminished 7 chords.

Look at the notes of C Whole-Half Diminished:

C D Eb F Gb G# A B

Contained within is a Cdim7 chord (C, Eb, Gb, A) and a diminished chord a half step below the root i.e. Bdim7 (B, D, F, Ab).

If we alternated between playing Cdim7 and Bdim7 arpeggios, technically we'd be playing the diminished scale.

Here's a lick where I play a Cdim7 arpeggio for four notes, then a Bdim7 arpeggio for four notes.

Example 7a

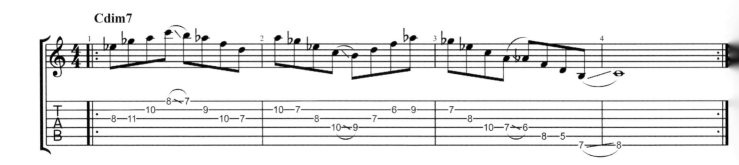

By thinking about the diminished scale in terms of chords, we're much more likely to approach it in a vertical fashion, rather than thinking of it as a linear thing. Taking the principle of what we just played and applying it, we can also take pairs of *triads* out of the diminished scale and use them to create melodic ideas.

And there are a *lot* of triads in the diminished scale. So many, that this chapter would be very long if I hadn't reined it in a bit!

Let's begin by looking at one of my favourite triad pair combinations from C Whole-Half Diminished, played over a B7alt chord. Over this chord I play a major triad from the root (B major) and pair it with a major triad from the b5 (F major).

Here are those triads played against a B7alt chord. You can mix up the notes of each triad. Notes from the B triad will sound very inside against the chord, and the F triad notes will sound outside.

Example 7b

If we combine those triads as a series of ascending 1/8th notes, then descend our diminished scale pattern, we end up with something that sounds really quite out there.

Example 7c

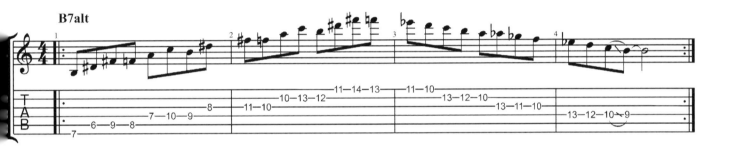

That last lick is a great one, but we're just ascending triads from the root note, so it could sound a little formulaic. If we know our triads thoroughly across the neck, however, we can play them in any inversion, like this.

Example 7d

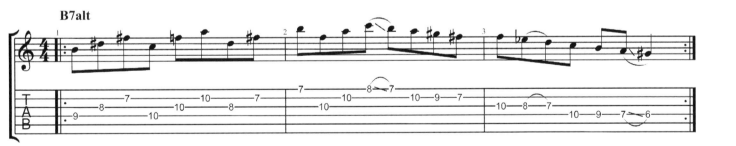

And, of course, we don't have to just ascend the triads. Here's a similar pathway, now ascending one triad then descending the next.

Example 7e

I'm a big fan of playing these triads in descending groups of three on the fourth, third and second strings which reminds me of the great Frank Gamble.

Example 7f

Now I'm combining those triads with the scale, but this time I'm using the scale in the middle of the run, rather than at the end.

Example 7g

We can also play to the strengths of the guitar and move the pattern up three frets. All the notes are contained within the C Whole-Half Diminished scale, but rather than looking for pitches, I've just learned where I can draw these triad patterns out of the diminished scale pattern I see on the neck.

Example 7h

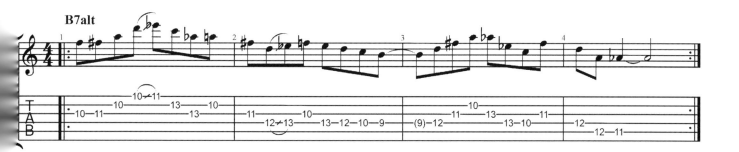

The beauty of this approach is that you don't always have to play all three notes of each triad to draw harmonic information from the chord. In this example I'm alternating between two notes of B major and two notes of F major. This disguises how the line is being constructed and makes it sound a lot less like a pattern, yet it still makes sense to the ear.

Example 7i

Here's the same idea moved up six frets, so that it starts around the F major triad alternating to B major. You can get a lot of mileage out of just this one triad pair!

Example 7j

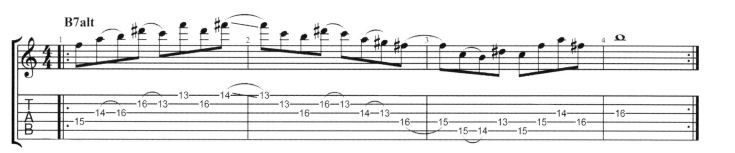

Let's move on to another triad pair we can extract from this scale. This time we'll use a minor triad played from the root of the B7alt chord (B minor) and pair it with a major triad from the 6th (G# major).

Played as ascending triads around the E shape of the chord, they sound like this.

Example 7k

There are limitless musical ideas to be had from this pair of triads too. Here's one that begins with a half step from D to D# – the 5th of the G# major triad.

Example 7l

I really like the first measure of that last lick. I play it quite often and shift it up in three-fret intervals, which sounds really cool. You just have to make sure you can resolve it!

Example 7m

We could take just the first four notes of that last lick and work with that idea too. I don't think of this as a pair of triads, but I know some great jazz players who would view this as a B minor and B major triad pair. When you move this up in three fret leaps it also sounds pretty cool!

Example 7n

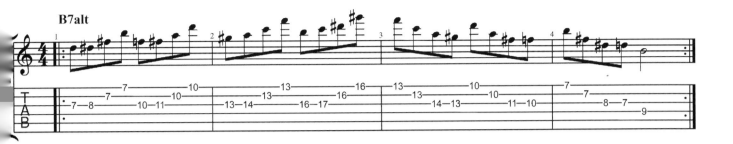

Your options for these triads are extensive and they'll all sound pretty interesting compared to just running up and down the scale. Here's a B major and D minor triad pair, played ascending.

Example 7o

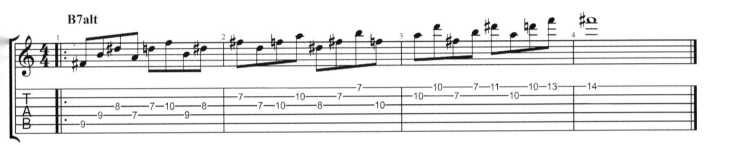

We can mix these ideas in any fashion – it doesn't need to be in groups of three playing all the notes of the triad each time. This lick is a real finger (and ear) twister, but we're still just drawing notes from those two triads.

Example 7p

Chapter Eight – Advanced Triad Concepts

We've looked at triad pairs, but now it's time to dig a little deeper and start combining multiple triads to create more complex sounding ideas.

We know that the easiest way to exploit the symmetrical nature of diminished ideas is to take patterns and shift them along the neck in minor 3rds. So, for example, over a G13b9 chord we might play an E major triad. But then we can shift that idea up the neck in three-fret intervals to give us E major, G major, Bb major and Db major, like this.

Example 8a

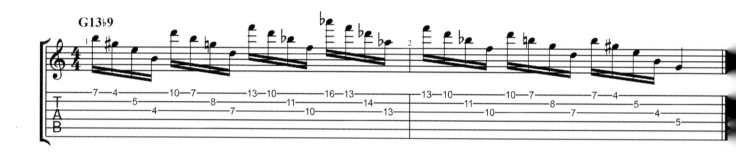

That's a very easy way to visualise the sequence. It becomes infinitely harder if we try to play the same triads in position. However, this does allow us to dress up the triads a little more, which makes them sound less like a pattern being repeated up the neck.

Example 8b

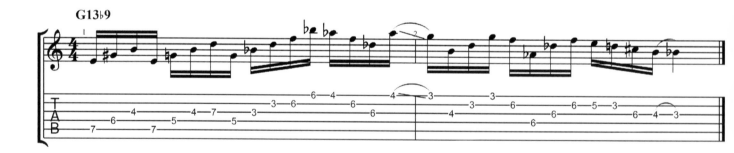

These two approaches aren't mutually exclusive, and one isn't better than the other. There's no reason why we can't take that last lick and move it up the neck as a symmetrical pattern!

Example 8c

That said, while it's possible to sit and compose very intricate ideas, to be able to use these concepts in an improvisational setting it helps to use triads anchored around chord positions that we play regularly.

If I lay them out around the E shape of G7, for example, we have this.

Example 8d

Here's the same idea, but now set around a C shape G7 chord.

Example 8e

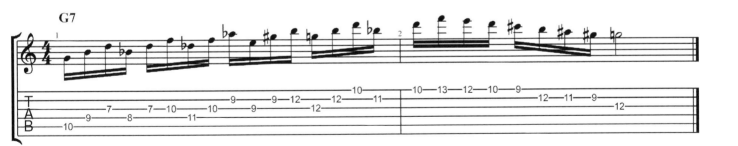

These triads become a different beast when we add an extra note to each of them, in this case a b7. This line is something you'd expect to hear from a player like Greg Howe.

Example 8f

In the previous example we added a b7 to each chord, but it works just as well to add a b3 to each triad.

Example 8g

The next example starts on the G root then ascends an E major triad, descends a Bb minor triad, ascends a G major triad, descends an E major triad, then ascends a Bb minor triad!

Example 8h

And here's one where we mix scalar runs with E minor, Db major, G major and E major triads.

Example 8i

Here's a third idea in the same vein that uses the G, Bb, Db and Eb major triads, mixed with some scale use.

Example 8j

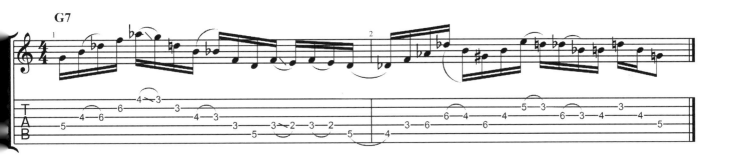

The real challenge is learning how to combine these triads fluidly anywhere on the neck. Here's an idea that starts in the C shape of G7 and moves down the neck.

Example 8k

Here's an idea up at the 12th fret area that begins with an ascending scale, descends an E major triad, then a Db major triad, and moves down the scale before ascending a Db7 arpeggio, then descending a G7 arpeggio.

Example 8l

Remember that you can always move these licks up/down in three-fret intervals. Here we move the exact same lick down a minor 3rd. The idea still works over the G7 chord but now we ascend the scale, descend a Db major triad, then a Bb major triad, play another scale fragment, then ascend a Bb7 arpeggio and descend an E7 arpeggio.

Example 8m

Here's a longer line that uses this combination of triads, but really mixes them up as we shift all the way down the neck.

Example 8n

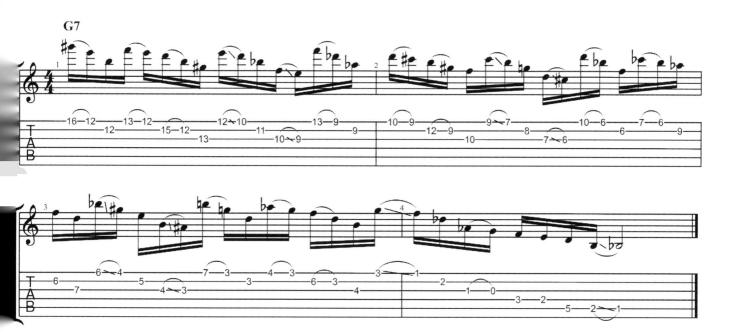

And here's one final lick that uses the same concept over a two-bar lick, then moves that idea down three frets to milk as much as we can from a single idea.

Example 8o

We've just played fifteen licks but as you can no doubt see, the sky is the limit with this stuff. We've looked at several different combinations and we've still only scratched the surface of what is possible with them.

From here it's a case of becoming more and more comfortable with how these triads fit together on the neck, then working on some of your own lines to bring out this wonderful sound.

Chapter Nine – Resolving Diminished Lines

We've covered a lot of diminished and dominant diminished ideas in this book, with the aim of helping you to freely draw from this sound in your playing. For most people, the appeal of a scale like this is that it creates an outside sound. It's something we play to extend the harmony from the diatonic into the realm of the weird and wonderful.

However, one of the most important things to understand about playing outside is that unless you play inside, there is no outside. Just as there is no dark without light, no big without small, and no sweet without sour, we must be able to play effectively inside to gain the full impact of going outside.

It's therefore important that we learn how to resolve our diminished lines, so we're able to move outside then back inside the harmony. In this chapter, our main focus will be resolving dominant diminished sounds up a 4th. Most often the resolution will be to a major chord, though you can resolve to a minor chord if you like.

You can achieve this using theory knowledge, but with practice you'll find that you're able to resolve your lines using a combination of your ears and muscle memory. The key is learning where the resolution points are located in your scale patterns.

Let's start by playing a B13b9 chord and resolving it to an Emaj7 chord. That's a V-I movement in E Major.

Example 9a

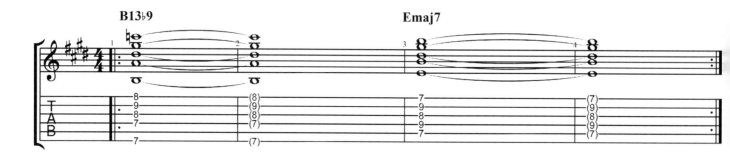

Now we'll play the same B13b9 chord, but in the second bar we'll add a descending scale run using the C Whole-Half Diminished scale (a.k.a. B Dominant Diminished). Then we'll resolve this run to the root note of the Emaj7 chord.

Example 9b

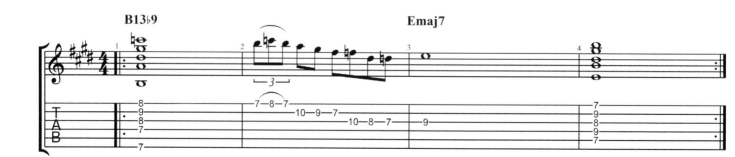

We can extend this idea by playing a two-octave line over both bars of the B13b9 chord, resolving to the root of the Emaj7 chord.

Example 9c

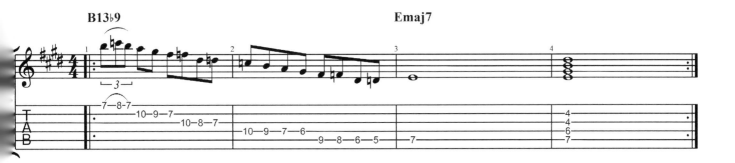

Here's the same idea, but now we add a melody over the Emaj7 chord. We started outside, but we resolved to the major chord.

Example 9d

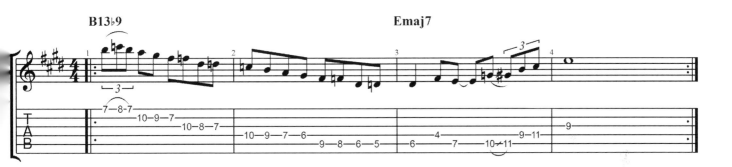

Our aim is to visualise any note in the Emaj7 chord and target it to resolve the line. Whenever I play a diminished idea, I'm more focused on where I'm going rather than where I am. So, here are two licks that resolve to the G# (3rd) of the Emaj7 chord.

Example 9e

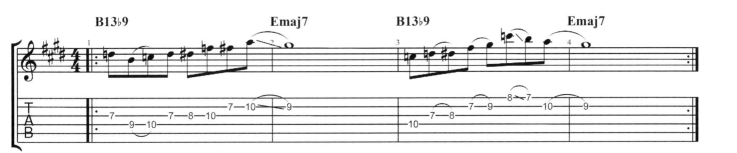

Here are two more ideas resolving to the same note.

Example 9f

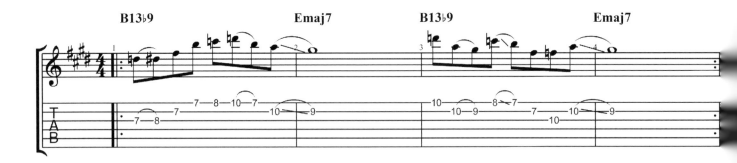

Now, here are two ideas that resolve to the B (5th) of Emaj7.

Example 9g

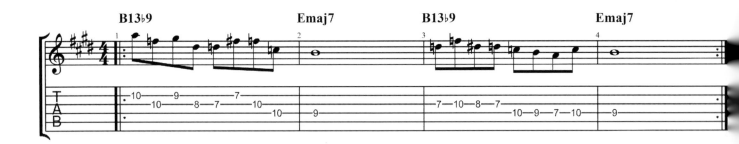

And another two resolving to the same note.

Example 9h

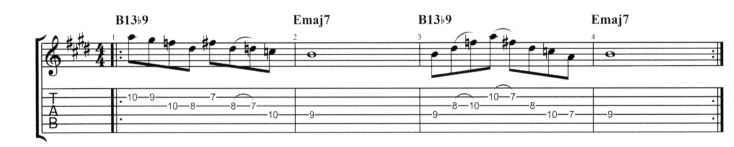

If we move our diminished scale to a different position (i.e. three frets lower), we'll have the same physical pattern, but the chord shapes underneath will change, which means our resolution points will also change. Now, our B13b9 to Emaj7 movement will look like this.

Example 9i

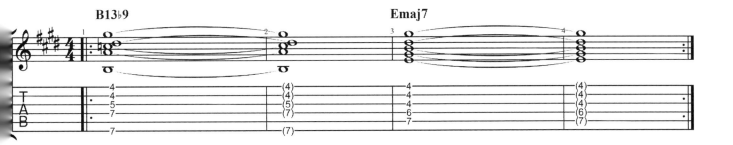

That means our arpeggios are going to look like this over those changes.

Example 9j

When we begin the play lines in this area, we're looking for different places to resolve. Here are two ideas that resolve to the G# of Emaj7.

Example 9k

Here are two ideas that resolve to the root note of Emaj7.

Example 9l

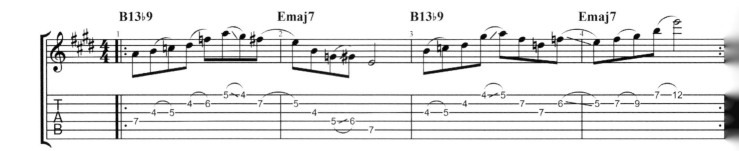

And two ideas that resolve to the 5th of the chord.

Example 9m

Once again, if we move to another position, we'll have the same physical scale shape, but our underlying chords and resolutions will change. Now, our movement from B13b9 to Emaj7 looks like this.

Example 9n

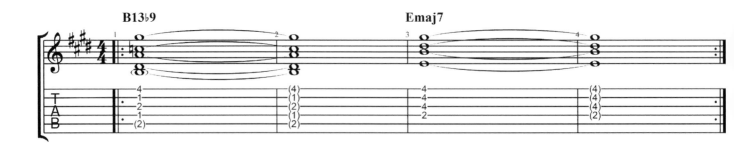

And here are our arpeggios connecting in this position.

Example 9o

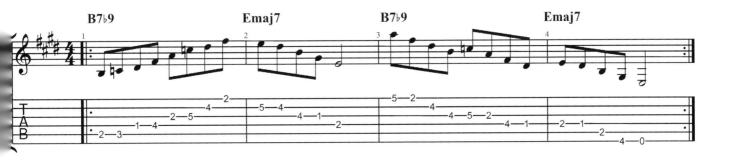

Here are two licks in that zone, resolving to the root of Emaj7.

Example 9p

And now two licks that resolve to the G# of Emaj7.

Example 9q

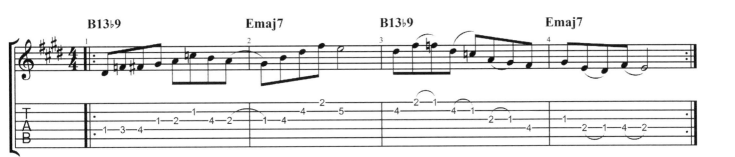

Next, two more licks, this time resolving to the B of Emaj7.

Example 9r

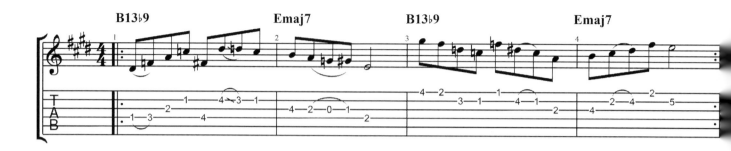

Finally, we can go back to our original position, move up three frets and we'll have another area to learn to resolve. Here's the new position as chords.

Example 9s

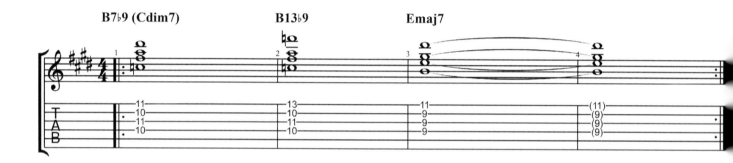

And as arpeggios.

Example 9t

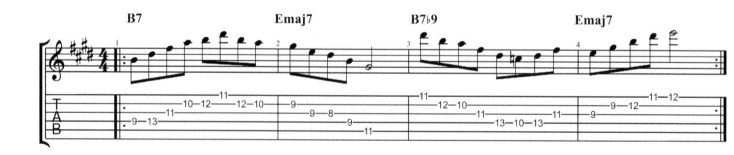

As long as we can "see" the Emaj7 chord, we can resolve our diminished lines. Here are two ideas that land on the root.

Example 9u

And two ideas where we land on the G#.

Example 9v

And, lastly, two licks resolving to the B.

Example 9w

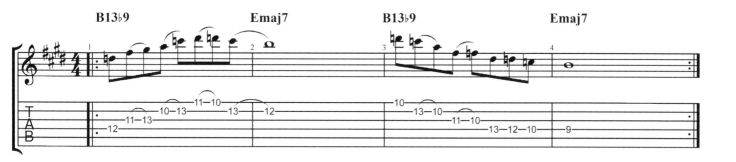

So, the key to resolving lines is to keep track of the chord you want to resolve to and visualise where its chord tones sit.

You'll have noticed throughout these examples, which covered four zones of the neck, that although we played the same physical diminished scale shape each time, the scale functioned differently. The nature of the diminished scale is that it always functions *four* ways.

We can use the C Whole-Half Diminished scale to outline the sound of a B13b9 chord, but the same scale also outlines D13b9, F13b9 and Ab13b9. That means we could resolve our diminished ideas not just to Emaj7, but also Gmaj7, Bbmaj7 and Dbmaj7.

This is why it's so important to keep the chord you're aiming for in focus. The symmetrical nature of the diminished scale is very inviting, but it's also like a merry-go-round – you need to keep an eye on where you're going to get off, because you can't stay on there forever!

Chapter Ten – Diminished Sounds… Just Because

Now we come to my absolute favourite way to use the diminished scale, and that is without any care or consideration for the *correct* usage.

As we've discovered, the diminished scale has a beautiful sound we can use to create rich harmonies like 13b9 chords, but those sounds don't crop up in music all the time unless you're a jazz musician. My main gig is a soul band, and my musical roots are in blues and early rock, so it would be useful if I could use some of these cool, outside sounds in ways that don't sound *too outside* for my genre.

Thankfully, there's a pretty easy way to do that!

As a blues-rooted musician, a lot of the phrases I play are based around the minor pentatonic and blues scales. Whether I'm playing Stevie Wonder's *Superstition* or Sam & Dave's *Hold On I'm Coming*, I'm going to be soloing with the trusty minor pentatonic. So, how can I use some of the ideas we've learned in this book in that setting, to bring a few wild sounds into that harmonically safe territory?

Simply put, I can just pretend I'm playing over a 13b9 chord even when there isn't one there. If I'm soloing in E Minor Pentatonic over Em7, for example, I can slip in and out of E Dominant Diminished (a.k.a. F Whole-Half Diminished) to imply the sound of E13b9.

This is really interesting to me. Everything I know about jazz tells me that when playing over a ii minor chord, we can imply its V chord in our lines to create tension and resolution. In this case, that would be a B13b9 moving to Em7. Now, B13b9 and E13b9 aren't the same chord and don't come from the same scale, so in theory this idea *shouldn't* work, yet it just does! That should remind us of our simple principle:

If the music sounds good, no explanation is needed. If the music doesn't sound good, no explanation will help.

Let's explore this idea in its simplest form. Here, we're playing an ascending E Minor Pentatonic scale, then at the top turning it into an E Dominant Diminished scale to descend, resolving to E Minor Pentatonic at the end.

Example 10a

Here's another way I might use the same concept.

Example 10b

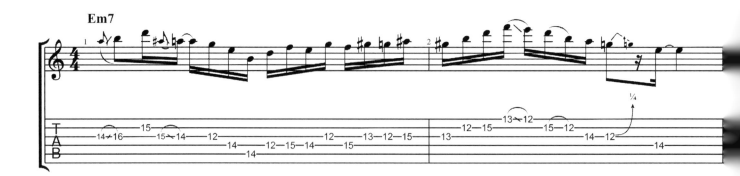

And here's a third idea. Again, we are just slipping out of the E Minor Pentatonic shape at the 12th fret, into the E Dominant Diminished scale, and back out again.

Example 10c

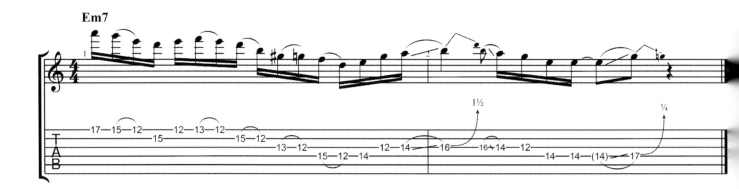

The magic of this concept is that once you've locked this pattern around your minor pentatonic patterns, you can replicate it anywhere.

As an example, here's a simple ascending and descending idea based around the 7th fret. This time I'll use the blues scale.

Example 10d

But I could do anything with these two patterns, like this lick, which I love to throw into my live solos.

Example 10e

Or this slippery little run that combines one of our sequencing ideas with a straight descending scale.

Example 10f

Now let's compare the sound we've been exploring to the common jazz approach of implying the V chord i.e. B13b9 resolving to Em7. Here is the same ascending E Minor Pentatonic scale, this time connecting to the B Dominant Diminished scale to conjure up the sound of the V chord.

Example 10g

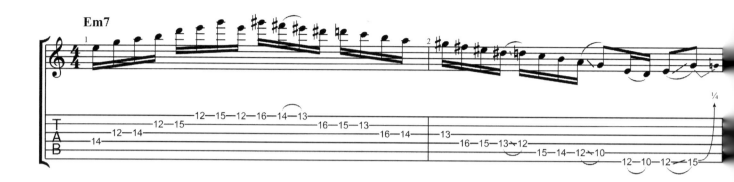

While you can absolutely play long scale runs like this, you can also just slip little fragments of the scale into the middle of a run to leave the listener unsure as to what just happened as it went by so quickly!

Example 10h

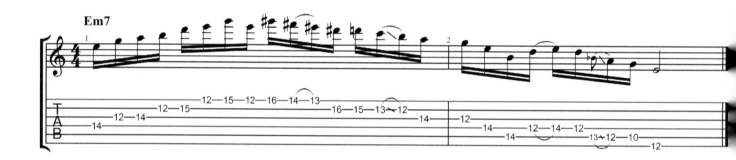

Essentially, we are using the dominant diminished scale here simply as a pattern, and the symmetry of the scale itself helps it make sense to the listener. Even if, according to theory, the notes don't fit, the ear can make sense of the idea because the scale is so logical.

This is a similar principle to the idea of playing a pentatonic "sidestep" lick, where we play a phrase, repeat it a half step above or below, then slip back into position. This idea shouldn't work either, theoretically, but it's not academic, it's music!

Example 10i

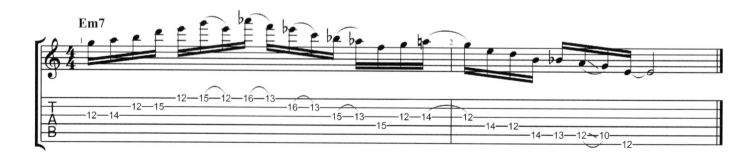

'll always remember the first time I heard the great Jimmy Herring playing his tune *Scapegoat Blues*. To me t's one of the greatest examples of a fluid combination of minor pentatonic and diminished phrasing. This next example is inspired by Jimmy. Here we start lower on the neck and move up, going back and forth between these two sounds.

Example 10j

Here's a lick that starts out using E Minor Pentatonic, then slips into the diminished framework with an E major triad and a Bbm7 arpeggio, before coming down a familiar two-string pattern.

Example 10k

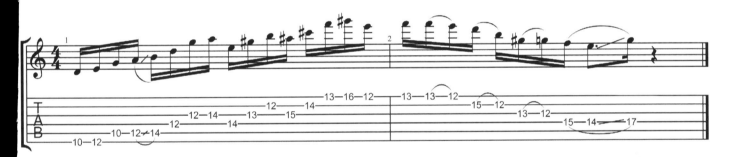

One of the things that became apparent in the advanced triads chapter is that there are a lot of chords that can be derived from the eight notes of the diminished scale. In that chapter we focused on triads, but if we add one more note, our options grow exponentially.

Here are four pretty wacky chords that Jimmy Herring uses on *Scapegoat Blues*. I've named them as logically as possible. Jimmy would call the second chord a Bb/B, and the third chord an Abm6#5, but when you know the diminished major 7 chord, it's much easier to spot!

Example 10l

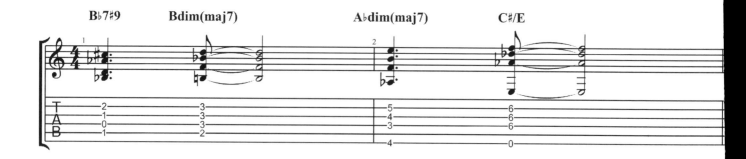

This groove is just a straight diminished vibe. Why? Just because! The thing I really want you to take away from this book is that while diminished scale sounds can be used in "correct" places, often the most versatile way to use the scale is simply as an exciting, jarring sound placed somewhere it doesn't technically belong.

To illustrate how Jimmy might use some of these outside sounds in his playing, here are four lines inspired by his style.

Example 10m

Here's a great one that uses a little more rhythm.

Example 10n

This idea takes one repeating symmetrical string skipping idea and moves it up in three fret intervals.

Example 10o

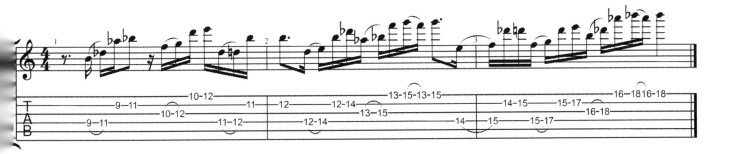

And here's one final lick that shifts up the neck as it progresses.

Example 10p

Conclusion – What's Next?

If you've made it this far, congratulations! You should now be in a place where you can play more than a hundred solid examples of the diminished scale sound on your instrument. But, of course, this is really just the beginning.

Much of the work in learning a scale is the process of shifting it from something you have to think about to something that's completely automatic – and the more harmonically advanced a sound is, the harder it will be to make it completely automatic.

I firmly believe this all comes down to listening. Music is a language and what (and how) we play is a product of what we hear. With any language, we imitate the things we hear, and we use the language in a way that makes sense in context. When we learn a new language, or just want to imitate an accent, it's no good just reading about it, we have to hear it and immerse ourselves in it.

That's trickier to do with the diminished scale because it's usually only a small part of a player's vocabulary. To make matters worse, we can't assume that everyone uses the diminished scale over dominant chords, because there are many other options. So, how can we do this?

You've already taken the important first steps. I'd like to think you've spent a good few weeks working through this book, and will spend several more weeks/months getting these sounds under your fingers and in your ears. That is really the only way you'll begin to discover this sound in the playing of the greats.

Aside from the great horn players like John Coltrane and Michael Brecker, and organists like Jimmy Smith and Joey DeFrancesco, you'll find diminished licks in the playing of numerous guitarists.

As a starting point there's Jimmy Herring, Oz Noy, Robben Ford, Larry Carlton, Mike Stern, Wayne Krantz and John Scofield to name a few.

Keep listening to these great players and when you hear something that sounds like the diminished scale, make a point of transcribing it. Were you right? If so, then work on absorbing that lick (and the context it was played in) into your playing as you practice. The more you work on this process, the easier it will become for you to spot this sound.

If you want to delve further into this subject, our own Eleonora Strino has a wonderful book that breaks down a lot of the great Barry Harris's method on the guitar. There are also further resources available from Don Mock (another fabulous player who loves some diminished ideas!) and Walt Weiskopf.

Keep listening, keep exploring, and I'll see you out there!

Good luck,

Levi

Printed in Great Britain
by Amazon

48884581R00051